1. Industry 1-40

2. Outliers 40-63

3. Advice/strategy 63-125

4. Conclusion and self-discovery 125-135

Chapter one: Industry

There has always been a tradeoff for tenancy - a fee paid to the "owner" for the land and its protection.[1] Today it is illegal to seize

---

[1] **Read more**: No Longer Nomads: The History Of Real Estate | Investopedia

someone's property by force. Research shows that it is not clear when the requirement for an individual who serves as a matchmaker between owner and buyer needed a real estate license. Some time in the late 1920's as mortgages and FHA housing rules came into play. Social inclusion motivated lawmakers to require licensing to prevent against discrimination. A real estate salesperson may sell mortgages.

    The connection between them says that if discrimination is carried out in the transaction then it should be punishable. Today we have a show "million dollar listing" that glorifies the job of an agent/salesperson to show a home. The show is on Bravo and will boost sales for the agents. Large real estate companies such as; Greystone, Keller Williams, Brown Harris Stevens, and others.

Barnett was born **Gershon Swiatycki** on the Lower East Side of Manhattan. His father Chaim Swiatycki was a rabbi and Talmudic scholar. He later moved to Monsey, New York. He received his Bachelor of Arts degree in

---

http://www.investopedia.com/articles/07/history-real-estate.asp#ixzz4QnBIMBoe
Follow us: Investopedia on Facebook

math from Queens College and received a Master of Economics degree from Hunter College.[1][2]

Career[edit]

Barnett began his career as a diamond trader in Antwerp, Belgium in the 1980s. In the 1990s, he returned to the United States to diversify into real estate, purchasing shopping malls and office buildings in the Midwest.[1] In 1994, he joined Kevin P. Maloney's Property Markets Group as a principal[3] and made his first New York City purchase, the Belnord apartment house.[4] In 1998, he built what would become the W Times Square. In 2003, Barnett partnered with the Carlyle Group to build The Orion, a 60-story luxury tower on 42nd Street.[1]

Barnett is a 2011 American Institute of Architects (AIA) Heritage Ball honoree. He also received the AIA New York Chapter Award in 2011.[5]

Barnett was ranked #6 on *The Commercial Observer*'s Power 100 list in 2011,[6] #2 in 2012,[7][8] and #1 in 2013.[9]

This is a piece of an article taken from wikipedia that talks about the founder of Extell Development. He is an outlier.

Born to a Jewish family,[3] Lichtenstein launched his real estate career with one building and a loan. And he bought that debut investment in a two-family home in New Jersey with a $12,000 down payment raised by maxing out a credit card and tapping out a small savings account.[1] Over the next couple of years, Lichtenstein used the cash his properties generated, leveraged with loans, to keep buying. Three years later, in 1988, he founded The Lightstone Group, quickly growing the company into one of the biggest private property holders in the U.S.[4] By 2003, Lightstone was recognized as one of the most active property buyers in the U.S., with an estimated worth of $1 billion to $2 billion.[1] By 2005, that worth had grown to an estimated $3 billion. David Lichtensteins story in unique. Gary Barnett spent time working with diamonds, this industry is a healthy place to meet wealth contacts.

The next important change was people in the US started viewing real estate as something that should be traded on the stock market. REITS were introduced as an investment tool that men could pool money together to contribute to a trust that would produce high volume returns. People who I hear about that make money through real estate do not use REITS.

Like all industry no wife will support you nor give you emotional motivation you may want. It must come from you. My words have no credibility because i am in the red financially.

I got licensed in real estate 1 year ago and my job has taken different expressions. In one office the alma mater of the company is make 100 phone calls a day and "please have six months of income in a padded expense account as a plan to live while working commision" said the CEO and COO to me. I sat at my desk and was vigilant to make my phone calls. I was taught how to use some software like "Propertyshark" and "Actovia" as well as how to say words a robot could utter.

My goal which was not stressed was to get an owner willing to allow us to sell his building that he had no prior expressed interest in doing. My goal to accomplish this was to question: "Are you looking to sell property "x"?".

As I will express later this is ineffective. Land is arguably the most valuable asset in one's life. So how would I with a question accomplish a transaction?

I was asked to leave the company for "being a nice guy but not a proper fit" within 1 week. I am disciplined and hardworking with little fear, so I was surprised and angry because I thought I would certainly do my time and make millions. My wife was expecting at the time and I wanted to support my family. What did they have to lose by having me on board? The pay structure would be 60% to the company and 40% to me if a transaction closed.

I have have been seated in multiple real estate offices so far and in my ignorance i see transactions closed by one of a few characters including real estate brokers with family ties to business, friends, and the outliers. I have had owners claiming to buy from me and mostly secretaries informing me that the owner is not buying or selling at this time. I have challenged secretaries to truthfully tell me if have a right to say that, the result was in one instance a affirmative no.

Currently owners tell me they are not selling. So where do all the daily real estate transactions come from if not those owner who told me they are not selling? Land is limited. Owners tell me "nobody is selling and the market is dead." The firm i am currently with tells me "don't worry about the number of calls just have a good conversation." This is good advice but I still have made no sales.

In real estate the agent sets the commission for the sale. Being licensed is not necessary because it only serves as a brief education with a test that ensure you will not discriminate and you will give disclosure. The latter sentence is a quote from my real estate instructor. Real estate is for the elite or those who had a strike of luck. The calls are boring and arduous.

In summary i got into the real estate business to make money and i like buildings. I am in withdrawal from these expectations that are not true for me.

The industry is a lie. I am lie too but it makes me uncomfortable that my impression of an office job was cognitive when it is more grating that working with a demolition team.

According to Choron.com, commercial real estate agents earned an average annual income of $90,000 as of 2013, according to the job site Indeed. This is significantly higher than the average income of $51,170 that the U.S. Bureau of Labor Statistics (BLS) reports for all real estate agents, including residential and commercial reps. However, BLS data is likely more skewed toward residential real estate agents, which explains the wide variance in salaries. Most commercial real estate salespersons have at least high school diplomas, but usually earn state-accredited real estate licenses before they obtain commercial real estate licenses. More employers are expecting these professionals to have associate's and bachelor's degrees. Independence, interpersonal and persuasive skills are highly desired traits of commercial real estate salespersons.

The statistic is not including salespeople in the first year of work. Most people I know made $0 in the first year of the job of a real estate salesperson. A blog i read on BOOMTOWN says that cold calling is now ineffective by just asking a question " are you selling your building now?"

Although i don't believe people who say things are ineffective i have found that while making a sales call i am calm and ask "are you looking to purchase a similar building to the one you own now?" This question provokes a response often such as, "what are you selling?" I still have only got one owner to tell me about a property he wanted to sell. The classic sales strategies about expanding clientele is irrelevant when comparing cold calling to get new clients. In theory getting a new client via phone is gotten through luck. Some people have been successful and selling a property to a client first before being given a sales listing.

Eliterealestaeprospecting.com states a story about a man who calls 197 people daily. Many real estate firms go by the 100 calls per day. Personally I am not lazy but half of the listed number on public record are incorrect and it takes time to prep 100 calls for a total of a 8 hours with one meal in between. This has not given me any listing especially since I am calling owner who are wealthy and asking would you like to part with your building?

I typed on amazon cold calling in real estate and the only 3 results were how to succeed in real estate without cold calling. The next part of the chain in business is the developers. I have worked for a developer while receiving a small salary. His business was not financially feasible so he closed. I have pursued both property management and project management jobs and I find that the level of safety among many general contractors are not to my satisfaction. For example a law was passed in New York that all construction must be viewed by a NY licensed superintendent, i heard about a contractor hiring a 70 year old man to sign off on projects he never saw. This man has a thriving business. This truth shows that in livelihood there is no justice!

All of the principles of Dale Carnegie's book are productive in cold sales. In the sales book written by Jeffrey Gitomer he discusses how Thomas Edison failed 6,000 times before creating the light bulb. This is great stuff that helps one to understand, persist, and create. The strategies are less about selling and more about psychological tips on life.

My thoughts is that this is precisely what sales represents today, a global view to open one to be able to receive pay for work. I may be great at these things but it is no guarantee that you will get paid for work. Someone may not be too good at sales strategy but make a nice living. Money is not given out in this world in a just way!

Classroom discussion is perhaps the most frequently used "active learning" strategy. However, instructors are often concerned about students who are less inclined to participate voluntarily. They worry that students not involved in the discussion might have lower quality learning experiences. Although instructors might consider whether to call on a student whose hand is not raised ("cold-call"), some instructors resist cold-calling fearing that the student will feel uncomfortable. This study examines the impact of cold-calling on students' voluntary participation in class discussions and their comfort participating in discussions. The results demonstrate that significantly more students answer questions voluntarily in classes with high cold-calling, and that the number of students voluntarily answering questions in high cold-calling classes increases over time. Furthermore, students in classes with high cold-calling answer more voluntary questions than those in classes with low cold-calling; this also increases over time. Finally, in classes with high cold-calling, students' comfort participating in class discussions increases while in classes with low cold-calling, students' comfort participating does not change.

Research findings show that cold-calling can be done fairly extensively without making students uncomfortable. Thus, the research reported here provides support for using this instructional strategy to engage more students to participate in discussions.[2]

This article shows that the more cold-calling is practiced the more the overall information gathering is increased. It is important to note that cold-calling is nothing more than questions and the more stimulation via questions is done the more engaged all parties will feel.

Citation

    Database: PsycARTICLES

    [Journal Article]

The Proactive Personality Scale and objective job performance among real estate agents.

    Crant, J. Michael[3]

---

[2] http://jme.sagepub.com/content/early/2012/05/04/1052562912446067.abstract

[3] http://psycnet.apa.org/journals/apl/80/4/532/

Journal of Applied Psychology, Vol 80(4), Aug 1995, 532-537.
http://dx.doi.org/10.1037/0021-9010.80.4.532

Abstract

1. A sample of 131 real estate agents was used to examine the criterion validity of the Proactive Personality Scale (T. S. Bateman & J. M. Crant, 1993). A job performance index was computed for each agent from archival records of the number of houses sold, number of listings obtained, and commission income over a 9-month period. Experience, social desirability, general mental ability, and 2 of the Big Five factors—Conscientiousness and Extraversion—were controlled for, and the Proactive Personality Scale explained an additional 8% of the variance in the objective measure of agents' job performance. These results provide additional evidence for the criterion validity of the Proactive Personality Scale and suggest that specific personality measures can have incremental

validity over the Big Five factors. (PsycINFO Database Record (c) 2016 APA, all rights reserved)

This article suggests that agent gain the skill of being proactive.

Journal of Applied Psychology 1995, Vol. 80, No. 4, 532-537 Copyright 1995 by the American Psychological Association, Inc. 0021-9010/95/$3.00 The Proactive Personality Scale and Objective Job Performance Among Real Estate Agents J. Michael Grant University of Notre Dame A sample of 131 real estate agents was used to examine the criterion validity of the Proactive Personality Scale (T. S. Bateman & J. M. Crant, 1993). A job performance index was computed for each agent from archival records of the number of houses sold, number of listings obtained, and *commission income over a 9-month period. Experience, social desirability, general mental ability, and 2 of the Big Five factors—Conscientiousness and Extraversion—were controlled for, and the Proactive Personality Scale explained an additional 8% of the variance in the objective measure of agents' job performance. These results provide additional evidence for the criterion validity of the Proactive Personality Scale and suggest that specific personality measures can have incremental validity over the Big Five factors. Attempting to predict job performance with personality measures has a long tradition in organizational research. This body of work has led some researchers to conclude that personality—relative to other predictors— is a rather weak predictor of performance (e.g., Hunter & Hunter, 1984; Schmitt, Gooding, Noe, & Kirsch, 1984). Recently, however, researchers have begun to reconsider the structure of personality (e.g., Digman, 1990) and the extent to which personality may validly predict on-the job performance (e.g., Barrick & Mount, 1991, 1993; Barrick, Mount, & Strauss, 1993). The purpose of this study was to examine the criterion validity of a recently introduced measure, the Proactive Personality Scale, by using objective job performance as the criterion measure. After discussing the theoretical underpinnings of the proactive personality construct, I review research pertaining to four domains that must be controlled in a rigorous test of the criterion validity of the Proactive Personality Scale: the Big Five factors, general mental ability (GMA), work experience, and social desirability. A version of this article was presented at the 54th annual meeting of the Academy of Management, Dallas, Texas. This research was partially supported by a grant from the Herrick Foundation. I thank Thomas Bateman and Edward Conlon for their helpful comments on earlier versions of this article. Correspondence concerning this article should be addressed to J. Michael Crant, Department of Management, University of Notre Dame, Notre Dame, Indiana 46556. Electronic mail may be sent via Internet to j.m.crant. l@nd.edu. Theory Development and Hypotheses Proactive Dimension of Personality Bateman and Crant (1993) discussed the proactive component of organizational behavior and introduced a measure of the proactive personality. This measure of a personal disposition toward proactive behavior is intended to identify differences among people in the extent to which they take action to influence their environments. Bateman and Crant denned the prototypic proactive personality as one who is relatively unconstrained by situational forces and who effects environmental change. Proactive personalities identify opportunities and act on them; they show initiative, take action, and persevere until they bring about meaningful change. In contrast, people who are not proactive exhibit the opposite patterns; they fail to identify, let alone seize, opportunities to change things. Proactivity is expected to be related to job performance because it represents personal behaviors that are important elements for accomplishing work-related tasks. Rooted in the interactionist perspective (Bandura, 1977; Schneider, 1983), the proactive approach considers the possibility that individuals create their environments. In the psychology and organizational behavior literatures, the theme of interactionism holds that behavior is both internally and externally controlled and that situations are as much a function of persons as vice versa (Schneider, 1983). Accordingly, individuals can intentionally and directly influence their situations, thereby making successful job performance more likely. More proactive people can be expected to create situations and 532 RESEARCH REPORTS 533 environments conducive to effective performance. Moreover, for some jobs, the creation of these environments is itself an element of effective job performance. How might real estate agents—the sample for the present study—exhibit higher job performance through proactive behaviors? One possibility is that proactive agents select environments conducive to effective job performance. For example, proactive agents might focus on the high-end market, thereby increasing one element of job performance: commissions generated. People can also initiate and maintain actions that directly alter the surrounding environment; proactivity is presumed to capture individual differences in this proclivity (Bateman & Grant, 1993). Thus, proactive agents might scour the classified advertisements of local papers for houses being offered for sale by owners and then solicit the owners to list their houses with the agent. They might carefully screen buyers to ensure that the agent works only with those ready and able to purchase a property. Proactive agents may advertise their services (often at their own expense) in an effort to generate new listings and clients. These proactive behaviors alter the environment by changing markets, clients, and marketplace perceptions of the agent. These are discretionary behaviors that are a function of individual differences in proactivity. Thus, indicators of agent performance such as commissions, listings, and sales logically would be higher for more proactive agents. Control Variables The Big Five model of personality. Over several decades, independent streams of systematic research into personality traits have converged on the same general conclusion: The domain of personality can be represented by five superordinate constructs (Digman, 1990). These general, robust factors of personality are known as the Big Five (cf. Digman, 1990; McCrae & Costa, 1989) and are at a higher level of abstraction than more specific personality variables. Thus, these factors are not intended to replace other personality systems; rather, they can be considered as a framework for interpreting other personality constructs (McCrae & Costa, 1989; Wiggins &Pincus, 1992). Although researchers do not agree on the labels assigned to the Big Five factors (Barrick & Mount, 1991), representative labels are (a) Neuroticism, or emotional instability; (b) Extraversion, described by being sociable, gregarious, and ambitious; (c) Openness to Experience, represented by flexibility of thought and tolerance of new ideas; (d) Agreeableness, represented by a compassionate interpersonal orientation; and (e) Conscientiousness, or the degree of organization, persistence, and motivation in goal-directed behavior. Two recent meta-analyses (Barrick & Mount, 1991; Hough, Eaton, Dunnette, Kamp, & McCloy, 1990) indicated that one of the five factors, Conscientiousness, is consistently related to job performance across all occupational groups. Extraversion appears to predict performance for jobs involving social interaction, like management and sales. The validities for the remaining three personality variables were somewhat smaller and differed by occupation or criterion categories. Thus, for many jobs, Conscientiousness and Extraversion appear to be the most relevant dimensions of the Big Five model. GMA. This measure has long been believed to be a key component of job performance (e.g., Hunter & Hunter, 1984; Schmidt & Hunter, 1981). In a meta-analysis on various predictors of job performance, Hunter and Hunter concluded that GMA is the single most valid predictor of performance for entry-level jobs. More recently, Schmidt and Hunter (1992) asserted that models seeking to explain job performance should incorporate both cognitive ability and conscientiousness. Work experience and social desirability. A thorough test of the criterion validity of the Proactive Personality Scale must also control for work experience. In their meta-analysis of various predictors of job performance for entry-level jobs, Hunter and Hunter (1984) found a mean validity coefficient of .18 for experience. After reviewing the work experience-job performance literature, Rowe (1988) concluded that work experience does enhance job performance. Finally, social desirability should routinely be controlled for in studies using self-report data. Social desirability may be considered as a style of responding that contaminates or distorts measures of personality. According to this viewpoint, a correlation between a social desirability measure and a personality scale compromises the integrity of the personality scale. Therefore, social desirability can be viewed as a nuisance variable that must be controlled for in studies using personality-based predictor variables (Nicholson & Hogan, 1990). Hypothesis On the basis of the discussion in the previous paragraph, it is reasonable to expect that experience, GMA, Conscientiousness, and Extraversion will be associated with job performance (social desirability is included as a statistical control). However, the Proactive Personality Scale is conceptually distinct from these other variables and has the potential to capture factors associated with job performance that are not accounted for by these other constructs. Thus, an effect for proactivity over and above the effects of these other variables is expected. In particular, after controlling for Conscientiousness, Extra- 534 RESEARCH REPORTS version, GMA, experience, and social desirability, I hypothesized that the Proactive Personality Scale would explain a significant amount of variance in objective job performance. Method Participants and Procedure The participants for this study were taken from 146 real estate agents in a medium-sized midwestern city. The average age of the sample was 47 years, and the average amount of real estate experience was 8 years. Fifty-six percent of the agents were women. The participants were drawn from four separate firms; the number of agents participating at each firm ranged from 10 to 79. 1 attended staff meetings at the four firms and administered a personality inventory, ability measure, and demographic questionnaire. Participants were asked to complete the materials as part of a study examining individual differences among real estate agents. The personality inventory and ability measure* are described below. The demographic questionnaire asked about the participants' age, sex, and number of years of experience as a real estate agent. The participants were assured of the confidentiality of their responses, and they returned the materials directly to me. I stressed that individual responses would not be seen by the agencies and would not be used to make any personnel decisions. To match the predictor and criterion measures, I asked participants to write the last four digits of their social security numbers on the questionnaires. Criterion measures were archivally obtained 10 months after the personality, ability, and demographic data were collected. The owners of the real estate agencies provided objective performance data covering a 9-month period for each agent who completed the earlier surveys. Among the 146 agents participating in the initial data collection effort, 8 agents terminated their employment during the job performance period and 7 failed to complete all of the items on the personality inventory. Thus, analyses were based on the 131 agents for whom all measures were available.

Measures Proactive personality. Proactivity was measured by using Bateman and Grant's (1993) 17-item measure. These items were summed to arrive at a proactive personality score. Responses are indicated on a 7-point Likert scale ranging from 1 (strongly disagree) to 7 (strongly agree). Sample items are "I excel at identifying opportunities" and "No matter what the odds, if I believe in something I will make it happen." Bateman and Grant (1993) presented the results of three studies assessing the scale's psychometric properties. Factor analysis and reliability estimates (ranging from .87 to .89) of the scale across three samples supported its unidimensionality. Convergent validity was demonstrated by means of moderate correlations with need for achievement and need for dominance. Proactive personality was not significantly associated with locus of control, providing some evidence of discriminant validity. To establish criterion validity, Bateman and Grant demonstrated that the Proactive Personality Scale was associated with involvement in proactive community service activities, the degree of constructive environmental change *revealed in essays of participants' most significant personal achievements, and with peer ratings of transformational leadership. Conscientiousness and Extroversion. These elements of the Big Five personality dimensions were each measured with a 12-item scale from the NEO Five-Factor Inventory (NEO-FFI; Costa & McCrae, 1992). The NEO-FFI is the short version of the NEO Personality Inventory (NEO-PI), which has been called the best measure of the five-factor model developed to date (Briggs, 1992). Costa and McCrae reported correlations between NEO-FFI and NEO-PI scales of .90 and .87 for Extraversion and Conscientiousness, respectively. The test manual provides evidence for the reliability (on the order of .90 and .78 for Conscientiousness and Extraversion, respectively) and construct validity of these measures. GMA. This construct was measured with the Wonderlic Personnel Test (E. F. Wonderlic & Associates, 1992), a timed, 12-min test of general g, the primary factor among the various factors that make up adult intelligence. Reliabilities reported in the test manual range from .88 to .94, and the manual also provides evidence for the validity of the measure. Social desirability. Social desirability response bias was measured with 10 items from the Marlowe-Crowne Social Desirability Scale (Crowne & Marlowe, 1960). Short versions of this scale have extensively been used in self-report data collection, with sound reliability and construct validity (Ballard, 1992). Job performance. The criterion measure for this study, job performance, was collected from objective archival data. After talking with the owners of the participating firms and reviewing previous research using real estate agents (e.g., Katerberg & Blau, 1983), I decided to collect information on three critical dimensions of each agent's job performance for which objective archival data would be available: the number of houses sold, the number of listings generated for the firm, and commission income. All measures were collected for a 9-month performance period. Results Because the three performance dimensions were highly intercorrelated (the correlation coefficients were as follows: sales-listings, .79; sales-commissions, .77; and listingscommissions, .70), z scores for each of the three performance dimensions* were computed and then summed to create an overall performance rating. Because two of the performance dimensions were stated in terms of the number of houses sold or listed and the third was in dollar terms, I used z scores to account for the measurement differences among the dimensions. In subsequent analyses I used the overall performance rating. Means, standard deviations, reliabilities, and correlations for job performance, proactive personality, Conscientiousness, Extraversion, GMA, experience, and social desirabil- RESEARCH REPORTS 535 Table 1 Descriptive Statistics and Correlations for All Variables Variable M SD \ 9 10 1. 2. 3. 4. 5. 6. 7. 8. 9. 10. Performance (z scores) Proactive personality Conscientiousness Extra version Neuroticism Openness to Experience Agreeableness GMA Experience Social desirability 0.00 90.79 46.69 45.81 27.89 38.62 47.01 24.91 8.37 6.08 3.00 14.04 6.78 6.37 8.22 6.67 6.13 5.73 8.97 2.03 (.90) .23** -.05 .01 -.10 -.11 -.11 .21* .28** -.06 (-89) .26** .35** -.12 .18 -.09 -.07 -.14 .09 (.80) .29** -.33** -.11 .40** -.14 -.06 .29** (.75) -.57** .15 .25** .04 -.29** .05 (.82) -.17 -.44** -.15 .16 -.32** (.63) -.02 .15 -.22* -.09 (.70) -.02 -.19*

.36** -.0—5 — -.09 -.10 (.72) Note. N = 131. Values in parentheses represent coefficient alphas. GMA = general mental ability.
*p<.05. **p<.01. ity are reported in Table 1. Although no effects were hypothesized for the other Big Five factors (Neuroticism, Openness to Experience, and Agreeableness), for completeness, Table 1 includes these variables. As shown in Table 1, experience had the highest validity coefficient among the predictor variables ($r = .28$, $p < .01$). The Proactive Personality Scale had the next highest validity coefficient ($r = .23$, $p < .01$), followed by GMA ($r = .21$, $p < .05$). The correlation coefficients between job performance and the other variables were insignificant. Social desirability was significantly associated with Conscientiousness ($r = .29$, $p < .01$) but not with proactive personality or Extraversion. To test the criterion validity of the Proactive Personality Scale over and above that of the other measures, I used a hierarchical regression procedure. Following the recommendations of Cohen and Cohen (1983), I entered the control variables into the regression equation before the proactive personality score.

Experience was entered into the regression equation in the first step, followed in turn by social desirability, GMA, Conscientiousness, and Extraversion. Finally, the proactive personality score was entered into the regression equation. The results of the hierarchical regression are displayed in Table 2. The results indicate that the Proactive Personality Scale does account for a significant amount of variance in the criterion measure, even when controlling for the effects of experience, social desirability, GMA, Conscientiousness, and Extraversion. Entering the Proactive Personality Scale into the regression equation explained an additional 8% ($p < .01$) of the variance in job performance. The effect was in the expected direction; agents with higher scores on the Proactive Personality Scale had higher job performance than their less proactive counterparts. Among the control variables, experience explained 8% of the variance in job performance ($p < .01$), and GMA explained an additional 5% of the variance ($p < .01$). To assess whether these findings held for each of the three dimensions of the overall performance rating, I computed separate hierarchical regression analyses for each of the three dimensions of job performance (sales, listings, and commissions) that made up the overall performance measure. After I entered the control variables, the Proactive Personality Scale explained a significant amount of the variance in each dimension of job performance. The effect was strongest for the number of houses sold (proactive personality accounted for an additional 9% of the variance in sales, $p < .01$), followed by commission income (7% of the variance, $p < .01$) and the number of listings obtained (6% of the variance, $p < .01$). Discussion The results of this study indicate that scores on the Proactive Personality Scale are associated with objective job performance, even when I controlled for the effects of experience, social desirability, GMA, Conscientiousness, Table 2 Results of Hierarchical Regression Analysis Overall performance rating Variable Experience Social desirability GMA Conscientiousness Extraversion Proactive personality A/?2 .076 .001 .052 .001 .008 .083 pof A .01 ns .01 ns ns .01 R 2 .076 .077 .129 .130 .138 .221 0

.329 -.011 .239 -.081 .007 .314 Note. GMA = general mental ability. 536 RESEARCH REPORTS and Extraversion. These results provide evidence that specific personality measures can have incremental validity over the Big Five factors. These findings are consistent with the interactional psychology perspective (Bandura, 1977; Schneider, 1983), which postulates that people influence their environments as well as vice versa. Individuals select, interpret, and alter situations. Evidence suggests that personality may be more useful in predicting behavior when autonomy is high compared with when it is low (Barrick & Mount, 1993), and the job of real estate agent offers considerable job autonomy. Thus, one explanation for these findings is that more proactive people tend to create situations consistent with effective job performance. When considering the generalizability of the findings, potential limitations should be noted. First, because the sample shared a single occupation, the results of this research probably should not be generalized beyond the real estate sales profession. Although it is possible and perhaps likely that similar results would be *found for other sales professions (e.g., stockbrokers, automobile and insurance sales, and manufacturing sales representatives), future research is needed to establish the generalizability of these findings. Second, in this study I used a sample of current employees. Future research might measure individual differences among job applicants to rule out the possibility that experience with the job itself affected the results. In the present study, I statistically controlled for experience. Regarding opportunities for future research, potential criterion measures appear unlimited (Bateman & Grant, 1993) and would vary as a function of the specific jobs studied. To more broadly assess criterion validity, researchers should study both subjective and objective measures (Muckler & Seven, 1992) of various dimensions of performance. The domain of dependent measures could be expanded beyond task-specific job performance. Other potential criterion measures include idea championing, innovation and intrapreneurship, whistleblowing, and certain types of organizational citizenship behaviors. Concerning control variables, because there is not uniform agreement on how to best operationalize and measure the Big Five factors, other measures (e.g., the Personal Characteristics Inventory [Barrick & Mount, 1993] and Goldberg's [1992] adjective set) should be included in future studies. In conclusion, this study provides some additional evidence for the criterion validity of the Proactive Personality Scale. The results suggest that the Proactive Personality Scale may be a valuable addition to the array of individual difference measures predictive of job performance. Although the research design did not permit statements of causality, the Proactive Personality Scale did account for variance in job performance over and above that accounted for by a number of other variables, including two of the Big Five factors. Thus, the Proactive Personality Scale is potentially useful as a selection or development tool. Future research is needed to establish its generalizability and boundary conditions. References Ballard, R. (1992). Short forms of the Marlowe-Crowne social desirability scale. Psychological Reports, 71, 1155-1160.*

Bandura, A. (1977). Social learning theory. Englewood Cliffs, NJ: Prentice-Hall. Barrick, M. R., & Mount, M. K. (1991). The Big Five personality dimensions and job performance: A meta-analysis. Personnel Psychology, 44, 1-26. Barrick, M. R., & Mount, M. K. (1993). Autonomy as a moderator of the relationships between the Big Five personality dimensions and job performance. Journal of Applied Psychology, 78, 111-118. Barrick, M. R., Mount, M. K., & Strauss, J. P. (1993, August). The joint relationship of conscientiousness and ability with job performance: A test of two theories. Paper presented at the annual meeting of the Academy of Management, Atlanta, GA. Bateman, T. S., & Grant, J. M. (1993). The proactive component of organizational behavior. Journal of Organizational Behavior, 14, 103-118. Briggs, S. R. (1992). Assessing the five-factor model of personality description. Journal of Personality, 60, 253-293. Cohen, J., & Cohen, P. (1983). Applied multiple regression/ correlation analysis for the behavioral sciences. Hillsdale, NJ: Erlbaum. Costa, P. T, Jr., & McCrae, R. (1992).

NEO-PI-R and NEOFFI professional manual. Odessa, FL: Psychological Assessment Resources. Crowne, D. P., & Marlowe, D. (1960). A new scale of social desirability independent of psychopathology. Journal of Consulting Psychology, 4, 349-354. Digman, J. M. (1990). Personality structure: Emergence of the five-factor model. Annual Review of Psychology, 41, 417-440. E. F. Wonderlic & Associates (1992). Wonderlic Personnel Test manual. Libertyville, IL: Author. Goldberg, L. R. (1992). The development of markers for the Big-Five factor structure. Psychological Assessment, 4, 26- 42. Hough, L. M., Eaton, N. K., Dunnette, M. D., Kamp, J. D., & McCloy, R. A. (1990). Criterion-related validities of personality constructs and the effect of response distortion on those validities. Journal of Applied Psychology, 75, 581-595. Hunter, J. E., & Hunter, R. F. (1984). Validity and utility of alternative predictors of job performance. Psychological Bulletin, 96, 73-98. Katerberg, R., & Blau, G. J. (1983). An examination of level and direction of effort and job performance. Academy of Management Journal, 26, 249-257. McCrae,

R., & Costa, P. T., Jr. (1989). More reasons to adopt the five-factor model. *American Psychologist, 44*, 451-452. RESEARCH REPORTS 537 Muckler, F. A., & Seven, S. A. (1992). Selecting performance measures: "Objective" versus "subjective" measurement. *Human Factors, 34,* 441-455.

Nicholson, R. A., & Hogan, R. (1990). The construct of social desirability. *American Psychologist, 45,* 290-292. Rowe, P. M. (1988). The nature of work experience. *Canadian Psychology, 29,* 109-115.

Schmidt, F. L., & Hunter, J. E. (1981). Employment testing: Old theories and new research findings. *American Psychologist, 36,* 1128-1137. Schmidt, F. L., & Hunter, J. E. (1992). Causal modeling of processes determining job performance. *Current Directions in Psychological Science, 1,* 89-92. Schmitt, N., Gooding, R. Z., Noe, R. A., & Kirsch, M. (1984). Meta-analyses of validity studies published between 1964 and 1982 and the investigation of study characteristics. *Personnel Psychology, 37,* 407-422. Schneider, B. (1983). Interactional psychology and organizational behavior. In L. L. Cummings & B. M. Staw (Eds.), *Research in organizational behavior* (pp.

1-31). Greenwich, CT: JAI Press. Wiggins, J., & Pincus, A. (1992). *Personality: Structure and assessment*. Annual Review of Psychology, 43, 473-504. Received March 23, 1994 Revision received June 20, 1994 Accepted August 1, 1994 [4]

In summary, the real estate sales industry has a lot to offer for those looking to grow in life skills. I will not make money but that is irrelevant to my work. I believe champions choose this profession. Especially in light of our sellers market. In addition all growth is hard.

---

[4]

http://www.optimizehire.com/wp-content/uploads/2013/05/Crant1995.pdf

Chapter 2: Outliers

In an interview for an assistant to CEO position which was nothing more than a desk and phone I was shown a newspaper of a man who closed a deal of 250 million dollars after 2 weeks in the real estate industry. Toward the end the interviewer told me there is no such thing as luck only 100 calls a day produces results. The amount of bullshit to this statement is enormous. There are people who do not make 100 call daily yet they make sales.

The outliers often have a two minds or powerful magnetism. "No better success like failure and success is not failure." says Bob Dylan, I feel like one of a kind in my industry but that won't make me successful. I am a qualified outlier because I have not closed one deal yet but i have the proper external disposition.

Advertising often plays a role in an agent's success. In my opinion this an elephant in a suit. They are outliers because they walk under the wing of a name simple branding. Fuck the big name people they cause much trouble as does anybody. Despite being broke I have made 100 calls daily and did not have a conversation. I would ask questions and the person whom i phoned would speak in short sentences. I also spoke with 4 people on some days and had conversations.

Another outlier is when the price payed for a property is out of proportion from neighborhood comps. To eat these sour grapes must be done, and to understand that the real estate broker field is dead except for the well established. Money is all luck and all words and action as futile as trying to prevent cancer.

I married my wife with little financial plans or more accurately no money and some personal debt. My plan was to use my wife's income which did not exceed 35k yearly. I went to study jewish law with the knowledge that this would not bring me income in this world. I was caught up in the enjoyment of it.

I got a contact inform me about a position to help find leases for marijuana dispensaries. I got paid 5000 dollars for this endeavor. My wife was pregnant at the time and expressed that we will need more money. I have worked many jobs and was willing to work but i wanted real money that would provide wealth, things that i am not accustomed to. I was not capable as i was when i was single to produce money.

Through this process I doubt my testosterone and other fears from the person i once was. I have become more calm and less aggressive. This may distract employers from seeing my progress. Perhaps i need real aggression to make a place for me to get money. Bring out the courage.

I am want to defend the weak. I am tired of desk bullshit and water cooler talk. I am the highway looking to use my gifts and abilities not sit and waiting without any pay. The challenge is great as my late dad did not provide me with a craft. I find my own role models now. I live day to day financially. My sense of qualifications of being an outlier is that i don't make money and work hard. I also feel so far away from money. Outliers only demonstrate relevance in the results! Often i feel emasculated because i live on my wife's money. I hate it!!!

Outliers such as Tupac and Biggie smalls die young. "Even though i sell rocks it feels good putting money in my mailbox." This raw action to make money is something i desire. Complacency bores me and i feel devalued. I feel enraged about this.

Studies show those who overachieve die young. I need to strike the world perhaps with great rhythm in drumming. One of my first passions was music. I need to release my power, the world will provide a tipping point. Real estate cold calls keeps me trapped not free.

I have multiple visible tattoos and that may be the reason of my lack of money. Sad but true that strong judgment is passed on petty shit as apposed to honor, courage, and commitment.

Some outliers stand out for their lack of family ties to business while others made a great financial move with property early in their career in real estate. It has been told to me by a friend that Warren Buffett gives credit to his father for his success because Warren was told from his father that he could do whatever he want's. I don't know the story of the salespeople to the left or right of me but it is likely that someone is an outlier. A real estate office manager told me that after years he almost closed a deal to find that it was taken from him. That sucks.

"a person or thing situated away or detached from the main body or system" this a definition of an outlier. So how should real people without background or family connections in real estate make money? It may be possible but it does not seem to be accomplished through cold calls.

Malcolm Gladwell states that 10,000 hours spend on a craft will produce results such as the work from Bill Gates. Depending on how many hours one commits this is between 2-3 years working long hours. I have heard from a family member about a guy who worked for 4 consistent years in real estate without making 1 deal. How did he wake up for 1,460 days and not think this is my fault? After all was he not in the wrong profession?

Did any friends and family still believe in the fourth year that he may make money? 10,000 hour rule states that he was putting in his time, so yes this is the norm.

Do people get paid in today's workplace for his/her innate talent or demonstration of hard work? It is crazy to think that no one gets paid money until doing 10,000 hours on a trade and having innate genius.

One contrast to the argument of the theory of outliers is that the feeling of belonging to the club of outliers is what is stated in the book Outliers by Malcolm Gladwell; he says that Jeb Bush who comes from a family of politicians considers himself a self-made man. If job success is determined by feelings of an individual than it is a great segway into my next chapter. I think perhaps people that feel bad for me will offer advice that produces no results that effect my wallet.

    In a show called "The west wing" there is a meaningful line expressing advice, a man in a hole sees a doctor walking by and asks would you please help me? The doctor writes a prescription and throws it in the hole. Later a priest walked by and the man in the hole asked the priest for help, the priest wrote some prayers on a paper and threw it into the hole. Finally a friend walked by and the man in the hole asked for help, the friend jumps into the hole. The man in the hole turns to his friend and says why would you do that, he responds by saying i have been here and i know the way out.

    The 100 job analysis: A job watching a dead body as its soul transcends to heaven. I said psalms around the hour in a funeral home.

    I worked as a manager of a bagel store that my counterpart was a man with a wife and kid and I was under 20 years old. I got proficient at the work and as i got money i purchased my first car. I had a sexual encounter with a girl of a different faith and this confused me.

I was a kitchen supervisor of a nursing home with 250 beds, the workers were union and i could not hire nor fire anyone. This caused me to leave with frustration.

I have had more jobs. I want to explain the phenomenon of the outlier and how there is no true outlier because much like a proton and neutron cause an extreme positive new force to be introduced.

American paratriathlete and former Paralympic swimmer Melissa Stockwell was the first female soldier to lose a limb in the Iraq War while serving her duty as a lieutenant. She lost her left leg in a bomb explosion when she was leading a convoy to Baghdad. She competed in the 100 meter butterfly, 100 meter freestyle and 400 meter freestyle at the 2008 Summer Paralympics as the first Iraq veteran chosen for the Paralympics. In her triathlon career after she moved from swimming, she won three consecutive gold medals in 2010

Budapest, 2011 Beijing and 2012 Auckland ITU Paratriathlon World Championships. Melissa was named USAT Paratriathlete of the Year in 2010 and awarded the Bronze Star and the Purple Heart for her service in Iraq.

    She channeled her disability become motivated. Motivation may come through positive or negative.

Teri Griege

Age: 54

Hometown: St. Louis, MO

Battling cancer didn't stop me from finishing the Ironman World Championship triathlon.

After my doctor told me I had stage 4 colon cancer, I set three goals: to celebrate 25 years of marriage with my husband, to live long enough to see my son and daughter get married and to compete in the

Ironman World Championship triathlon race in Hawaii. With only a five-year survival rate of 6 percent, I knew the odds were against me, but I wasn't going to give up on my dreams.

Two years after hearing my diagnosis and still receiving chemotherapy, I found myself setting up my transition area in the dark morning hours of what would become my most memorable race day ever.

Getting to Kailua-Kona, Hawaii, wasn't an easy journey. I went through radiation treatment and multiple rounds of heavy chemotherapy on top of several surgeries to resect areas of my liver and colon. But even while enduring the toughest of times, it was my desire to live that kept me fighting.

As I treaded water in the Pacific Ocean, waiting for the iconic cannon fire to signal the start of the race,

I looked over to see my family happily waiting to cheer me on. In that moment, I reminded myself that my purpose for the day wasn't to be fast; it was to finish what I started and hopefully inspire others along the way.

After gliding through the 2.4-mile swim, I ran through the transition area, where I hosed off the saltwater. Grabbing my bike, I set out on the 112-mile course with the mindset of taking one mile at a time.

Though the bike course was tough with rolling hills and strong headwinds, seeing my support crew—35 of my closest friends and family had come to support me— helped energize my legs and spirit to continue.

Relief filled my body when I came to the end of the bike portion and changed into my running shoes for the last leg of the race. Heading out on the island's famous Ali'i Drive, I soaked in the moment while watching the sun set across the ocean. As my legs continued carrying me forward, I reflected on the experience I was living, feeling so blessed and grateful to be alive.

I stuck to my plan of running from aid station to aid station, which helped chunk the 26.2-mile distance into manageable pieces. During the last few miles of the run, I heard the finish-line party and felt it drawing me closer with every step.

Running through the chute, I was overcome with emotion. I crossed the line with a total time of 14:50:32 and flew into the open arms of my mother, husband, two children and oncologist. In that moment, I knew it was possible for dreams to come true.

While some might say I finished one of the biggest endurance events in the world that day, I know fighting cancer is my greatest race. I will continue to arm myself with the lessons Kona taught me. I will endure and always have hope that life continues after the finish line.

Running taught me to fight for my dreams. Build an army of support, and your potential is limitless. I'm still receiving chemotherapy every other week and might be for the rest of my life, but I now know that anything is possible as long as I'm powered by hope

[5]

She show that the impossible for some will be done. I imagine many doctors told her

---

[5] http://womensrunning.competitor.com/2016/07/inspiration/stage-4-cancer-ironman_62327#wIiLkotm0DyYM6eF.97

not to do compete in Ironman. Possibly that may be why she did it, to defy odds at all costs.

      These goals were not accomplished for financial gain rather personal satisfaction. I believe this is more attainable than money. I don't get paid but i do challenge myself by working for free as well as being in a marriage where i am the receiver. Many forms of personal satisfaction are not achieved through recognition.
      In a book titled Rebels in the holy land, the author discusses jewish farmers from Poland who left their families to start a farm to sustain people in Israel. These pioneers around the year 1870 defied many odds to accomplish the goal. Often someone with a disability will accomplish despite the attached opinion. I am sure people do not think i will be rich but that has no impact on my working for free now. True confidence sits in my stomach that i am challenging myself and resting at times.

Abstract

A survey revealed that researchers still seem to encounter difficulties to cope with outliers. Detecting outliers by determining an interval spanning over the mean plus/minus three standard deviations remains a common practice. However, since both the mean and the standard deviation are particularly sensitive to outliers, this method is problematic. We highlight the disadvantages of this method and present the median absolute deviation, an alternative and more robust measure of dispersion that is easy to implement. We also explain the procedures for calculating this indicator in SPSS and R software.

      This is a novel approach to calculating when someone is an outlier, rather than looking to see if someone stands out of the average we should look at the middle number to see if someone stand out. This lowers the concept of outliers to be a valid study.

Untangling performance from success

- Burcu Yucesoy and
- Albert-László BarabásiEmail author

EPJ Data Science 2016 5:17
DOI: 10.1140/epjds/s13688-016-0079-z
© Yucesoy and Barabási 2016
Received: 18 January 2016
Accepted: 20 April 2016
Published: 29 April 2016

Abstract

Fame, popularity and celebrity status, frequently used tokens of success, are often loosely related to, or even divorced from professional performance. This dichotomy is partly rooted in the difficulty to distinguish performance, an individual measure that captures the actions of a performer, from success, a collective measure that captures a community's reactions to these actions. Yet, finding the relationship between the two measures is essential for all areas that aim to objectively reward excellence, from science to business. Here we quantify the relationship between performance and success by focusing on tennis, an individual sport where the two quantities can be independently measured. We show that a predictive model, relying only on a tennis player's performance in tournaments, can accurately predict an athlete's popularity, both during a player's active years and after retirement. Hence the model establishes a direct link between performance and momentary popularity. The agreement between the performance-driven and observed popularity suggests that in most areas of human achievement exceptional visibility may be rooted in detectable performance measures.

Keywords

success performance popularity

1 Introduction

Performance, representing the totality of objectively measurable achievements in a certain domain of activity, like the publication record of a scientist or the winning record of an athlete or a team, captures the actions of an individual entity [1, 2, 3, 4, 5]. In contrast success, captured by fame, celebrity, popularity, impact or visibility, is a collective measure, representing a community's reaction to and acceptance of an individual entity's performance [6, 7]. The link between these two measures, while often taken for granted, is actually far from being understood and often controversial and lopsided. Indeed, even the most profound scientific discovery goes unnoticed if its importance is not acknowledged through discussions, talks and citations by the scientific community. The void between success and performance is well illustrated by the concepts of 'famesque', 'celebutante' or 'faminess', used to label an individual without tangible performance, but 'known for his well-knowingness' [8]. These often prompt us to see fame and success as only loosely related to [9, 10, 11] and often divorced [11, 12, 13, 14, 15, 16] from performance. This dichotomy is illustrated by documented examples of scientists whose popular media visibility significantly exceeds their scientific credentials [17], or by countless celebrities, from the Kardashian sisters to athletes with no or only underwhelming accomplishments [18, 19, 20], as well as by high performers like David Beckham or Tiger Woods who are frequently featured in the media for reasons unrelated to their professional achievements [21, 22]. The source of this dichotomy is that in most areas of human achievement it is difficult to distinguish performance from success [23]. Indeed, while we can use citations, prizes and other measures to quantify the impact of a scientific discovery, we lack objective performance measures to capture the degree of innovation or talent characterizing a particular paper or a scientist.

Our goal here is to explore in a quantitative manner the relationship between performance, an individual measure, and success, a collective measure capturing the societal acknowledgement of a given level of performance. Previous research, some using Google search results as a proxy for fame, have suggested that performance can indeed drive success [24, 25, 26, 27, 28, 29, 30, 31]. Here, by exploring the timelines of both achievement and its recognition, we uncover how performance affects success over the career of an individual. We do so through sports, an area where performance is accurately recorded in terms of number of wins, place in rankings or career records [32, 33, 34, 35, 36, 37, 38].

Sports is characterized by an equally obsessive focus on popularity and fame, which strongly affects an athlete's market value [39], and previous research shows that fame can be an appropriate proxy for accomplishment [40]. Yet, in sports too, performance and success often follow different patterns, illustrated by the fact that only a small fraction of the earnings of a professional athlete is tied directly to his/her performance on the field, the vast majority coming from endorsements, determined more by the athlete's perceived success and popularity. For example, only $4.2 million of Roger Federer's $56.2 million reported 2014 income was from tournament prizes [41], the rest came from endorsements tied to the public recognition of the athlete. Yet, Novak Djokovic, who was better ranked than Federer during 2014, received over $12.1 million prize money but only $21 million via endorsements, about a third of Federer's purse. The fact that professional performance does not uniquely determine reward is further illustrated by Anna Kournikova, who in 2003 was the second best paid female tennis player, despite never reaching higher than the 8th place in rankings. Her popularity and consequential financial prowess is often attributed to her photogeneity and media-friendly personality, traits outside of her sports performance. This and many other well documented cases of 'faminess' raise an important question: What performance factors affect popularity and how do they do so? In other words, can performance explain popularity and fame and if so, to what extent? These are fundamental issues in most areas that aim to fairly reward excellence, from science to education and business.

While we would like to believe that fame, visibility and popularity are uniquely determined by performance, representing well-deserved recognition for some sustained or singular achievement, a significant body of media research indicates otherwise, suggesting that fame follows patterns on its own, divorced from talent or performance [8, 9, 10, 11, 12, 13, 14, 15, 16, 17, 18, 19, 20, 21, 22]. Here we aimed to quantify the relationship between performance and popularity in an area where these two quantities can be individually measured. We did so by constructing a model to predict a tennis player's visibility captured by his Wikipedia page-views, a proxy of the athlete's popularity and fame. Taken together, we find that in tennis a player's popularity and momentary visibility are uniquely determined by his performance on the court. The agreement is especially good for elite players. This indicates that for athletes exceptional performance offers exceptional visibility, a level that is hard to modulate by exogenous events. For less accomplished players we observe deviations from the performance-predicted popularity, suggesting that in this case visibility can be manipulated by exogenous events or personal attributes outside of the scope of sports performance. It is comforting, however, that for most outliers the extra visibility can be explained by performance factors not considered in our model, like achievements in doubles or junior tournaments. In short, the better the performance of an athlete, the more accurately it determines his popularity, and the lesser the role of exogenous factors. Finally, we find that the fame of retired players is also determined by their past performance, indicating that exceptional past performance can lead to a commensurate lasting legacy.

We expect that our methodology can be readily generalized to other areas where performance and visibility can be independently measured. The generalization to sports like chess, table tennis, golf or car racing should be straightforward as the ranking systems of these sports are similar to tennis. With careful adjustments it may also be appropriate for team sports, allowing us to systematically explore how the performance of a professional athlete is tied to his/her or the team's collective success.

We would like to believe that in most areas of human achievement fame and visibility are determined by some underlying performance indicators. The scientific challenge, however, is to systematically separate performance from success, a fundamental goal from science to management. The excellent agreement between the performance-based and the observed popularity documented here makes us wonder to what degree faminess is real, suggesting that outstanding fame and popularity may be rooted in performance measures that are perhaps not yet accessible to us.

      This article precisely identifies something i see pervasive across all financial matters. The input will not guarantee output reinforcing that justice is not the way of the world. Media, advertising, and many other factor may play a role in one's financial status.

Chapter 3: Advice/Strategy

    This chapter is about the kind but false words of advice. The first piece of advice i got was you won't make money in real estate. The first job i took told me "i don't think this field is for you."
    The second perl of advice is that the economy sucks. I have been told by an owner that the key is to know the deal well this advice works best if I got listings. All work is hard but people talk as though real estate is especially difficult in the beginning. In my experience working as a restaurant manager and US Marine all work sucks. As soon as arriving into work I want to leave. Knowing that would get paid some day was motivating but not for long as now i have volunteered my time for free. Or played lotto tickets. I just make my call because it is what i do without the eagle screaming.

I grew up in a family with multiple teachers including my father and mother. I am one of seven children. I do not agree with their life choices personally. They do not complain at all to me.

My late father never discussed work with me that i could recall in the 23 years i knew him. I worked since I was 11 years old. I have friends who observe my work that i do and despite being in the red financially they say i am inspiring with my determination. Some friends have given me real estate connections that produced no financial gain.

I have worked with the disabled for one year and got paid for it. My mother has seen my work and now tells me "why don't you just do similar work", this is faulty because for years I have been looking for a position in this field. My mother is 70 years old and she has the worked the same job since she graduated college over 30 years ago. She must think it is up to me if i get paid. I don't believe it is up to me if i get paid. I have built my confidence up to trust in GOD that i will get paid, this building of trust took 5 years of practice. I was let down by being in the red for 1 year consistently now.

I have had real estate owners tell me that i need to get listing directly from sellers to be successful. They claim that they have been in my position. I have been told by one of my brothers to take an aptitude test with an organization that help people locate appropriate jobs for individuals. I emailed them. I am not confused as to what i want to do, i just want to get paid!

  I have interview in 1 year for 10 jobs. I think of myself as someone living in the great financial depression. Studies show that women in their 20's are more likely to get hired and get paid more than men in their 20's. All this adds up to advice and it consistently just lets me down. I now have no expectations minus the fact that i most likely will not get paid forever. I still seek work and make cold-calls for work.

  I have a female cousin close in age to myself who works as a business recruiter. She graduated Bentley University and found a job shortly after and no unemployment interruptions. Nepotism is responsible for many of the people I see with a job currently, but in a vacuum nepotism in not the complete answer because it is man's job to seek work regardless or under what conditions.

  Self-help and tips come in the form of books and people talking. It is a billion dollar business that all forms under the auspices of advertising. They all cost money and provide entertainment but share a personal story that works for an individual from amongst 6 billion people. Despite advice just being entertainment i have experienced motivation and hope to move on in my sales from a kind word or piece of personal experience from a friend or colleague.

An important reality that I observe among those who are employed with a salary job is he/she has some kind of following. For example someone who owns an apartment building will often have a manager, super, and many others looking for employment including real estate and mortgage brokers.

A rabbi who is the leader of a congregation will have followers. These people give validation to this man to the public view which attracts others and many opinions. The notion that a man could succeed without a reputation today is scarce and in of itself is an outlier.

A partial motivation to write this book is to dispel from myself the notion that I am alone and if a by product will be my being know, that is a bonus. Any part of the person that is famous I have found is surface deep to his/her true identity. For example a famous boxer is known among people for his boxing credentials.

Once an employer sees some external credentials the more desirable one becomes. Here is an example, upon graduation, Einstein could not find a higher education teaching post. The father of a (nepotism)classmate helped him obtain a job as a technical assistant examiner at the Swiss Patent Office in 1902. He obtained his doctorate after submitting his thesis "A new determination of molecular dimensions" in 1905.

The science career of Albert Einstein really took off in that year, 1905. He wrote four articles that provided the foundation of modern physics. The papers were on Brownian motion, the photoelectric effect and special relativity. He won the Nobel Prize for physics in 1921 with the paper on the photoelectric effect.

Tom Cruise might get a lead role while a more talented actor will not just because of a label. Although this theory has truth I don't believe it the reason for my lack of getting paid currently. I have had a 5 years lapse in employment due to personal choices one of which was to go study in a post-high school higher talmudic studies school. What I got from the school in valuable but not job affirming.

My thoughts about my own getting paid is that it won't happen for me but it won't stop me from trying. Another point i touched upon in my journey thus far is that an employer often feels more qualified to take the position i am interviewing for thereby leaving me at a disadvantage. I am competing with age, status, and experience rather than skill.

The rule of irrelevance: A stockbroker was interviewing me for a position in his company and when he saw my short sleeve short he and his partner has mention of it when I started work i should wear long-sleeve shirts tucked in. External professionalism in the form of clothes may be important if something is at risk in this case I would be a day-trader working from a desk, in short often people give back-handed admonishment or suggestions to bring success when they had no real application.

I believe people only use part of their brains when interviewing someone.

Although a college degree has been sold to Millennials as a surefire ticket to high-paying jobs, many recent college

graduates are finding they can't get jobs that pay much more than minimum wage.
One reason for the difficulty is college is a bad place to get career advice. After all, tenured professors haven't hunted for a job in decades while adjunct professors get paid peanuts.

Not surprisingly, colleges provide very bad advice to graduates looking for their first job. For example, here's a direct quote from a UC Davis guide on presenting yourself to a prospective employer:

> "An elevator speech is a clear, brief message or 'commercial' about you. It communicates who you are, what you're looking for, and how you can benefit a company or organization.
>
> "It's typically about 30 seconds, the time it takes people to ride from the top to the bottom of a building in an elevator. (The idea behind having

an elevator speech is that you are prepared to share this information with anyone, at anytime, even in an elevator.)

"At a career fair, you can use your speech to introduce yourself to employers. It is important to have your speech memorized and practiced. Rehearse your 30-second elevator speech with a friend or in front of a mirror.

"The important thing is to practice it OUT LOUD. You want it to sound natural. Get comfortable with what you have to say, so you can breeze through it when the time comes."

Here's why this advice is so awful:

1. *People hate commercials.* People spend billions of dollars worldwide every year on streaming video in order to avoid commercials. Why would you think a hiring manager would want to hear a commercial?
2. *People hate sales pitches.* The entire idea of a sales-pitch-like elevator pitch is ridiculous. If you actually launched into a sales pitch in an elevator, the other person would hit the next floor button and leave. A conversation, maybe, but not a pitch.
3. *People hate memorized speeches.* Only some droning professor could possibly imagine anyone wants to hear a rehearsed speech, especially a sales pitch. As for the idea that you can "breeze through it" -- ugh. Sounds like the Home Shopping Network.

The UC Davis guide then gives some examples:

> "Hi, my name is Samantha Atcheson, and I am a senior environmental sciences major. I'm looking for a position that will allow me to use my research and analysis skills. Over the past few years, I've been strengthening these skills through my work with a local watershed council on conservation strategies to support water quality and habitats. Eventually, I'd like to develop education programs on water conservation awareness. I read that your organization is involved in water quality projects. Can you tell me how someone with my

experience may fit into your organization?"

"Nice to meet you, I'm Alex Biondo. I'm currently a senior and am studying computer and information science. I hope to become a computer programmer when I graduate. I've had a couple of internships where I worked on several program applications with a project team. I enjoy developing computer applications for simple business solutions. The position you have listed in UO-JobLink seems like it would be a perfect fit for someone with my skills. I'd like to hear more about the type of project teams in your organization."

Here's my translation of the examples above:

> "ME ME ME ME ME ME ME ME ME ME ME ME ME ME ME. But enough about ME! Let's talk about what you can do for ME!"

No wonder college graduates can't find good jobs!

Rather than this kind of claptrap, college students should be taught the rudiments of selling as it's done in the real world.

An elevator pitch, for example, is not a 30-second block of motor-mouthing. Effective elevator pitches consist of three answers to three implicit buyer questions:

1. The benefit (answers "What's in it for me?")
2. The differentiator (answers "Why buy it from you?")
3. The call to action (answers "What's the next step?")

An effective elevator pitch is delivered conversationally, rather than as a speech, like so:

- Exec: "So, Brad, what are your plans?"
- Brad: "I convince Millennials like me to begin investing when they're young." (Benefit)
- Exec: "How do you do that?"
- Brad: "Because I'm a Millennial, I understand what motivates my peers." (Differentiator)
- Exec: "That's interesting. What motivates them?"
- Brad: [after providing an anecdote that illustrates the differentiator] "It sounds like you might be interested in hiring somebody who could attract successful young investors."
- Exec: "Yes, that's in our plans."

- Brad: "We should talk. What's the best way to get on your calendar?" (Call to action)

As you can see, this elevator pitch is focused on the needs of the buyer (i.e., the hiring manager) and introduces the candidate's experience only as proof of the candidate's ability to deliver.

Savvy readers will realize immediately the same thing is true of all sales and marketing messages. If your message is about YOU, it's the wrong message.

Like this column? Sign up to subscribe to email alerts **and you'll never miss a post.**
The opinions expressed here by Inc.com columnists are their own, not those of Inc.com.

This is an example of people discussing a solution that does not work for me. In my real estate sales i ask if If I could sell property or buy from an owner. It is not about me. The generation older than millennials have expectations that do not match my personality not skills.

One moment in the third Republican presidential debate encapsulates everything terrible about baby boomers and the way they've pillaged the U.S. economy. It came from Sen. Marco Rubio of Florida, a Generation Xer, who offered the standard line — you can hear it from the mouth of almost any American politician today — on how to keep Medicare and Social Security solvent. Rubio defended the idea that future workers will need to retire later or receive fewer benefits from those safety-net programs than current retirees. "Everyone up here tonight that's talking about reforms," he stipulated, was "talking about reforms for future generations. Nothing has to change for current beneficiaries."

That's smart politics: The biggest generational voting bloc by far in the upcoming election will be baby boomers, a group that is just starting to draw its first Medicare and Social Security benefits — and does not want anyone messing with those benefits, thank you very much.

It's also bad economics.

Boomers soaked up a lot of economic opportunity without bothering to preserve much for the generations to come. They burned a lot of cheap fossil fuels, filled the atmosphere with heat-trapping gases, and will probably never pay the costs of averting catastrophic climate change or helping their grandchildren adapt to a warmer world. They took control of Washington at the turn of the millennium, and they used it to rack up a lot of federal debt, even before the Great Recession hit.

[Baby boomer nostalgia is already oppressive. It's about to get so much worse.]

If anyone deserves to pay more to shore up the federal safety net, either through higher taxes or lower benefits, it's boomers — the generation that was born into some of the strongest job growth in the history of America, gobbled up the best parts, and left its children and grandchildren with some bones to pick through and a big bill to pay. Politicians shouldn't be talking about holding that generation harmless. They should be asking how future workers can claw back some of the spoils that the "Me Generation" hoarded for itself.

When you look at the numbers, the advantages boomers have enjoyed are breathtaking. Start with the economy. Boomers went to work in a job market that their children rightly romanticize. It delivered living-wage work for wide swaths of Americans, even those who didn't go to college, which by the way cost a fraction of what higher education costs today, even after you adjust for inflation. A single earner could provide for a family. Employees could reasonably expect to advance in their companies and work their way into the middle class. Incomes grew across the board.

Earlier this year, in a paper for the Brookings Institution, economist Robert Shapiro tracked the lifetime earnings paths for Americans who entered the labor market in the 1970s, 1980s, 1990s and early 2000s. He found a sharp generational divide. The typical U.S. household headed by someone who was 25 to 29 years old in 1975 saw its real income increase by 60 percent until it peaked and began to slowly decline before retirement. For a similar household in 1982, lifetime income peaked 70 percent higher than its starting point. Those are both boomer cohorts.

The groups that came after fared worse. Workers who were 25 to 29 in 1991 saw median earnings peak 50 percent above where they started. For the 2001 group, the peak was just over 20 percent higher. (Though there's still time, theoretically, for their earnings to rise again.) For both those groups, the high point came much earlier in their working lives than it did for the boomers.

My generation, Gen X, is in far worse financial shape than our parents were at the same age. Millennials are even worse off than we are. Soon after the Great Recession ended, the Pew Research Center reported that middle-class families were 5 percent less wealthy than their parents had been at their age, even though today's families work a lot harder — the average family's total working hours has risen by a quarter over the past 30 years — outside the home, and even though they're much likelier to include two wage earners. The ensuing recovery has made things worse. Middle-class families owned fewer stocks, businesses and homes in 2013 than they did in 2010, according to calculations by New York University economist Edward Wolff.

[Quiz: Can you match the generalization to the generation?]

Meanwhile, future generations will have to pay the costs of weaning the world from fossil fuels and/or adapting to warmer temperatures, rising seas and more extreme weather. (Estimates vary, but some projections suggest they could total trillions of dollars for America alone.) They will also have to shoulder the burden of keeping America's retirement promises to the boomers. The Congressional Budget Office estimates that the rising costs of Social Security and government health care that will stem from an aging population will consume two more percentage points of America's economic output by 2040. If policymakers don't find the revenue to pay for it all, the CBO projects that the national debt will climb past 100 percent of annual gross domestic product — quadruple its post-World War II low.

And yet almost no one suggests that boomers should share the pain of shoring up those programs. Folks my father's age like to say they've paid for those benefits, so they should get them in full. But they haven't. The Urban Institute has estimated that a typical couple retiring in 2011, at the leading edge of the boomer wave, will end up drawing about $200,000 more from Medicare and Social Security than they paid in taxes to support those programs. Because Social Security benefits increase faster than inflation, boomers will enjoy bigger checks from the program, in real terms, than their parents did.

The sin here isn't exactly intentional: It's not boomers' fault that there are so many more of them than their predecessors (their ranks peaked near 80 million, some 30 million more than the Silent Generation before them) or that they're living longer (retirees today can expect to live three or four years longer than their grandparents). The sin is that boomers have done nothing to ameliorate their easily foreseen threat to the U.S. Treasury. They have had every opportunity: Congress has been controlled by a baby boom majority since the beginning of the George W. Bush administration.

Did that majority sock away money for future safety-net costs? No. Pols talked about putting budget surpluses in a "lockbox," but not for long. Instead they cut their own taxes, they deficit-financed two wars, they approved a new Medicare prescription drug benefit that their generation will be the first to enjoy in full. Partly as a result of those policies, the federal budget deficit has averaged 4 percent of GDP in the Bush/Obama era, more than double the average rate of the 50 years before that. Boomers let federal debt, as a share of the economy, double from where it was in 1970.

[Grandparenting 101 for baby boomers]

Meanwhile, they stood by while the economic bargain that lifted them as young workers began to unravel for their children. They opened global trade and watched millions of

U.S. manufacturing jobs vanish; research by MIT economist Daron Acemoglu and colleagues suggests that normalized trade with China, the biggest driver of those losses, has by itself cost America at least 2 million jobs.

Then, boomers didn't invest enough in new training programs for young workers, particularly men, who once could count on factory jobs to bring them a middle-class lifestyle. They allowed college costs to more than double from 1982 to 2012. Though, point in their favor: Many of them took out loans to send their children to school.

Boomers let public investments in research and development — a critical driver of future prosperity — fall steadily as a share of the economy; they're down from 1.2 percent of GDP in 1976 to 0.8 percent today, a decline of one-third. In the 15 years boomers have been running Congress, economic growth has slid well below the average of a generation ago — to 1.9 percent a year, down from 3.2 percent for the preceding 25 years. Some of the brightest minds of their generation built fortunes working at Wall Street investment banks, then helped drive the economy into its worst recession since the Great Depression.

It's increasingly clear that Generation X, and possibly millennials, haven't learned from the boomers' mistakes. My son will rightly criticize me someday for my generation's love of SUVs. He'll probably wonder why he has to pay higher taxes or work several more years just to get a retirement that's worse than my dad's or maybe even mine.

Every generation wants to leave a better world for the ones to follow. I truly believe that boomers had no idea, for a long time, that the sum of their choices — of their quest to make life as good as it could be for themselves — might be a worse world for their children. But it's apparent now.

Those words were from the Washington Post.

Corporate mission

What is the point of focusing on these non-traditional hiring topics? Two letters – X and Y. Generation X (born between 1963 and 1980) and Generation Y (born after 1980) are establishing a more prominent position within the employment landscape as the Baby Boomers prepare to exit the workforce. The shift to these younger generations is prompting a new focus in hiring tactics.

The Baby Boomer generation was cut from the cloth of work first and foremost, climb the corporate ladder and retire with a healthy pension plan. Those days are all but gone. Today, younger workers are creating a paradigm shift in employee hiring based on their priorities. We have observed this accelerating transition firsthand over the past two years.

We work with companies in many market spaces, industries and geographic locations. The hiring landscape has already changed and companies that do not frequently hire may be unaware of the new focus. Certain patterns exist today that are universally consistent when hiring Gen X and Gen Y employees.

Work-Life Balance

Perhaps there is no more profound shift in values than this topic. Gen X, and even more so Gen Y, is focused on a position's time requirements. This isn't to say the younger generations are not hard workers. On the contrary, they put tremendous effort into their work, but they also place a high value on their personal time away from the office. This balanced approach has been mistakenly interpreted by the Baby Boomers as a "slacker mentality".

The younger generation's search for opportunities where they can grow their skill set without having to sacrifice every other area of their life. As an employer, it is imperative to understand this desired balance. Positions that lack the needed support, tools or technology often will be a red flag to the Gen X or Y candidate. The reward for accepting such a position clearly has to outweigh the perceived imbalance it may cause in their life.

Skills Path

Most people are familiar with the term "career path". The Baby Boomer generation experienced a marketplace where preordained opportunities existed to climb the corporate ladder within the same company. Today's younger generations generally do not have such consistent opportunities before them. More importantly, many of the younger generation do not subscribe to the same loyalty as the Baby Boomers.

Gen X and Y candidates are looking for a "skills path". They desire to understand what skills are needed to be successful in the position today. The long-term incentive is to understand what skills they will personally develop or acquire within the company. They prefer a horizontal management structure and respond to personal skill development. Titles are out. Responsibilities are in. It is imperative to share with the candidates the responsibilities they will inherit as their skills become more advanced over their tenure with the company.

Sherpa Managers

As mentioned, the younger generations have a fairly horizontal view of the org chart – whether accurate or not. We have seen this approach wreak havoc in an office dominated by Baby Boomers. The Baby Boomers expect an almost military-style chain of command while the younger generations have a more fluid approach to positions of authority.

Gen X and Y highly value the manager-employee relationship. They view their manager as a guide – an experienced Sherpa to make sure they are on the right path. In debriefing Gen X and Y employees after they are hired, the vast majority consistently mention the impression of their manager as having the most influence on their decision to join the company. The hiring manager needs to connect with the Gen X and Y candidate on a personal level during the interview process. Clearly the manager-employee relationship is a two-way street, so this approach affords the hiring manager a beneficial insight into the candidate also.

Work Smarter Not Harder

These generations are plugged-into technology from Bluetooth to Blackberries. They have spent much of their working careers, even entire lives for some, having Internet information available to them at a moment's notice. This fact can work against employers in that these younger candidates are savvy about Internet job boards and have a tendency to always have an eye out for new opportunities.

However, the upside of this technological ability is far greater. A subtle item we have observed among Gen X and Y candidates is their strategic thinking. Their youthful age belies the fact that they have sharp minds for understanding macro markets. We have seen these younger candidates ask amazingly insightful questions that make the hiring managers pause during the interview. We have also seen strong candidates pass on opportunities because they were skeptical of the hiring company's shallow business plans.

The Gen X workforce will be ascending into prominent management positions at a brisk pace over the next five years. The next wave of change will occur in the management ranks as they shift the hiring process away from the Baby Boomer approach. The aforementioned topics will move to the forefront of the hiring process as the newly crowned Gen X managers hire the Gen Y employees. Until that happens, progressive companies will perceive these current shifts and adjust their hiring tactics in advance.

Businessperform.com is responsible for this great insight that demonstates the difference between a much antiquitated approach (military style) to a more open and understanding approach that understands that millennials have new rescources that Baby boomers(1946-1964) did not. Recruiter earn 50k plus and it as a job that revolves around finding jobs for others.

In an Adecco survey of hiring managers, 75 percent said millennials' biggest interview mistake was dressing inappropriately, and almost as many said they tended to mess up by posting inappropriate material on social media. Almost two-thirds of respondents said millennials tend to demonstrate a lack of research preparation for interviews. These hiring managers also said they were three times as likely to hire a worker over age 50 as a millennial.

I may have not always dressed the most appropriately because i found that this does not help! The hiring manager says a disturbing thing "3 times more likely to hire someone 50" the reason for this could be a simple mistake that we are all guilty of, respecting age. Without any true skills attached age should be irrelevant.

New York Daily News write Michael Levin published this article to demonstrate a strong stereotype. I interviewed with all 3 generations and I am desperate to make money to feed my wife and son.

As God is my witness, I will never hire a millennial again as long as I live.

Much has been made of the so-called millennial work ethic.

I'm convinced these people want to have jobs — they just don't want to work.

Admittedly, they have a healthier attitude toward work than my generation.

They fit work into their lives instead of scrambling to fit their lives around work, as do people my age.

The problem is that when they actually get to the office, nothing happens.

I've been through four different admins in the past year and a half, and each was worse than the previous one.

It's hard to tell if they can't do the work or if they just simply don't want to.

A look at the literature suggests that there are many reasons why millennials are so diffident about their role in the workplace.

Most struggle with large amounts of student debt.

Maybe they figure that there's so little hope of reducing that debt, based on their entry-level salaries, that they give up before they start.

The whole point of an entry-level salary is that if you stick around, the salary moves up as your responsibilities grow.

As the expression goes, your raise becomes effective the moment you do.

Last month, I hired a twenty-something admin with great credentials and outstanding references.

Two weeks later, I had to send her an email pointing out the sloppiness and inattentiveness in her work product and requesting a better level of effort.

I'm not talking about anything insane — just getting phone numbers and time zones correct. "Easy button" kind of stuff.

That very same day, she sent me an email reminding me that she had a bachelorette trip to Florida in three weeks that would cause her to miss three days of work.

Who takes vacations two months after they start the job?

Who has the tin ear to put in a vacation request the same day the boss sends you an email about sloppiness?

Millennials, that's who.

People who study these matters suggest that millennials grew up in a culture where everyone was made to feel special.

You didn't have to put forth an effort to win a ribbon or even a trophy.

Just showing up was good enough.

What a terrible lesson to teach young people.

I don't mean that adults should pace Patton-like in front of small children and inform them that the world doesn't owe them a living.

And yet, the world owes no one a living.

My soon-to-be former admin ignored being fired and prepared to come to work the following Monday, George Costanza-like.

So I had to fire her a second time.

This time, she finally understood that I meant business, and that she was out of the business.

She responded with a plaintive email reminding me that without her job, she no longer had a source of income. Did I have any ideas about how else she could make money?

Then she asked if she could list her position with my company on her resume and use me as a reference.

You cannot make this stuff up.

Last time I checked, jobs that pay more than $50,000 a year as a starting salary and include health insurance aren't that thick on the ground.

Ironically, she had been my second choice candidate for the job.

My first choice was a woman with an even more stellar track record.

Unfortunately, when I performed a cursory Google search of her name, I found photos of her on websites like sexilicious.com — you can look it up — where she expressed the fact that her greatest desire in life was to become a plus-size model.

I have no problem with the fact that she wants to be a plus-size model.

Everybody has dreams.

I don't have a problem with her being a plus size.

I struggle with my weight, too.

I do have an issue with the fact that my clients could Google her and find the same compromising photos I did.

They would also see the terrible grammar with which she described her plus-sized dreams.

The final straw came yesterday, when my millennial bookkeeper announced in an email that she was leaving "effective immediately" and would have nothing further to do with my company. She wouldn't even share passwords with her successor.I'm sorry, millennials. You're all special. You're all smart.

And you're all fired.

Call it age discrimination. Call it self-preservation. Call it whatever you want.But if you're under 30, the unemployment office is two doors down

The following is an article courtsy of Telegraph.co.uk

Millennials have hit Peak Moan CREDIT: JENNY MATTHEWS/ALAMY

- Alex Proud

21 DECEMBER 2015 • 9:04AM

A Little over a decade ago, I had a member of the baby boomer generation sit me down and tell me the world didn't owe me a living and that I should stop being such a whiny, entitled crybaby.

Unsurprisingly, at the time I didn't appreciate it and, equally unsurprisingly, I later realised he was right.

So, as a member of Generation X, I now feel it's time to pass the baton on. Millennials, Generation Y: many of you are now in your 30s and it's time to grow up and stop whining.

This hasn't come entirely out of the blue. Rather it was "triggered" (to use a very millennial word) by reading a blog by a woman in her early 30s. She was talking about wanting children and how she didn't feel financially secure enough and couldn't buy a house.

Regular readers of this column will know that generally I have a great deal of sympathy for those priced out of the housing market and indeed, in the first few paragraphs, I felt pretty sorry for her.

But as I read on my sympathy started to ebb. The woman, you see, wanted to be an author of hipsterish Brooklynite novels. Her bloke wanted to be a musician or an artist or something.

She kept contrasting her life situation with her parents' relative good fortune. And pretty soon, I was thinking, "The reason you don't have everything your parents did is because you and Mr Blogger want to be *artistes* whereas your dad was probably a middle manager at IBM."

University students tend to stand in front of - rather than behind - the bar CREDIT: FRESH MEAT

Of course, we've all been here. My Generation-X contemporaries thought for a while that we could make a living telling each other stories of groovy modern alienation and ennui. In the end, it turned out only Douglas Coupland could do this. Personally, I thought I could run photography galleries.

This was a really cool lifestyle (I met a lot of celebrities) but it was a truly terrible job (I earned less than a trainee accountant). So, eventually, most of us grew up, stopped feeling sorry for ourselves and found proper jobs. We found fulfilment via screaming children, overpriced exotic holidays and new Farrow & Ball colours. We made our peace with the man and realised that, if you substitute Vietnam for Italy, we're basically OurParents2.0.

The boomers worked hard to enjoy their time CREDIT: BBC

Millennials are now at peak moan. Yes, we've been here before - but I do think that millennials are moaning louder and longer than Gen X or the boomers.

Whether it's jobs, property, or just the sheer towering unfairness of the world, millennial complainants are everywhere, ready to give you a rundown of everything their generation has been stiffed on. In the way that we once had The Greatest Generation, we now have The Whiniest Generation.

But really, the only place they've been short-changed compared to us Xers or even the Boomers is property. And even that isn't nearly as black and white as they'd like to think it is.

OK, let's start with jobs. Many millennials are weirdly perfectionist about work in a way that we Gen-Xers just don't get. There's a role at my clubs which involves booking bands. If you want to get into the music industry it's a great job. You can do it straight from university and it's a proper position with a salary, not an internship.

You get to deal with people in music every single day. And yet, I've seen people leave it time and time again. It's not like they have to speak to me on a day to day basis and deal with my inconsistency as a boss, so what gives?

They'll usually say that it's not what they expected. But what they did expect? And then you realise: they expected it to be like *Almost Famous* and they're really pissed off when it isn't. They expected the job to be some fabulous groovy extension of their Shoreditch lifestyle, but actually it's work.

To many millennials, this seems to come as a genuine surprise. It shouldn't: the clue is in the name. This isn't just my experience either: there's plenty of research that suggests millennials think that jobs should suit them, rather than the businesses that pay their salary.

One such study from the university of New Hampshire found "these employees have unrealistic expectations and a strong resistance toward accepting negative feedback."

I sometimes wonder if the millennial belief that your job has to be some great passion or calling or lifestyle accessory comes from never having known a real recession. Yes, I appreciate we are still living with the effects of the global financial crisis but I'm talking about a recession with proper, massive unemployment. The kind of recession that made you glad to have any job at all, like the one my generation graduated into, **which came hard on the heels of an even tougher** one.

We Xers may be associated with slacking but we're actually pretty tolerant of non-dream jobs. Working in Waterstones for two years while dreaming of a graduate position at Unilever will do that to you.

Anyway, let's move on. Property. The big one, if you live in London or the South East. Yes, I agree that the property market sucks for you. But while those of us born before 1975 had it pretty good, we didn't have it quite as good as you think.

When you look at that older friend who has a four-storey townhouse in East London or a loft in Hoxton that they bought for peanuts in 1995, what you're forgetting is that they had to live there between 1995 and 2005. And my God, sometimes these were pretty horrible places to live.

My generation tend to trot out war stories about living in rough neighbourhoods in the 90s with a dash of bravado, but often it really wasn't very nice at all.

"The modern equivalent of picking up a loft in Old Street

circa 1996 would probably be going to buy a big house in some run-down part of Manchester or Hastings"

Alex Proud

Quite a few of them couldn't take it. I have friends who got in too early in the gentrification cycle and had to move out again. The reasons? Little things like gangland executions a few doors down (trendy Hoxton); having your car burnt when you complained about the noise (hip Brixton); being burgled multiple times while you slept (groovy Clapton); or just deciding that a rape in your street doesn't have much cachet (cool Bethnal Green). As someone said to me the other day, "Yes, this house cost peanuts in 1997, but for years you had to take a cab to the train station, which is a three minute walk away." (newly fashionable Lewisham)

These areas were a far and very bleak cry from the spruced-up adult playgrounds that you see today and the people who moved in back then were real pioneers.

They didn't protest against Tesco's opening - they prayed for them. The modern equivalent of picking up a loft in Old Street circa 1996 would probably be going to buy a big house in some run-down part of Manchester or Hastings. And I don't see many of you queuing up to do that.

What about the rest? Well? It's not just jobs and property. There's plenty of lifestyle whining too. There's your newfound PC-on-steroids which leads you to rail against free speech at universities, demand safe spaces and airbrush the parts of history that upset you.

I'm afraid us oldsters just don't get this. We had exactly the same history as you and I don't think it ever occurred to us that walking past a statue of someone who'd been dead for hundreds of years created a threatening atmosphere. History's full of bad stuff: stop moaning, get over it and be glad you're not a peasant in 1400 or a soldier in 1915. Or, for that matter, a Syrian today.

Then there's the inability to take criticism that has led my fellow X-er, Bret Easton Ellis to brand you "Generation Wuss." Ellis's theory is that, even more than our generation, Gen Y have been coddled and showered in praise and given stars for just showing up. "What we have is a generation who are super-confident and super-positive about things, but when the least bit of darkness enters their lives, they're paralysed," he told *Vice*.

I'm with Ellis here. I used to think many of my contemporaries were spoiled, but millennials seem to have elevated First World Problems to an art form. And yes, I do think they've been wrapped in cotton wool in a way previous generations weren't.

We grew up in the 80s which were kind of horrible. There was a sense of class hatred, a sense of decline and the UK felt like a failed country. The only places that recapture that feeling these days are the bits of Eastern Europe that still haven't got over communism.

"The second you let go of the idea of having a perfect job or a loft in Shoreditch or the idea that the oppressive statue at uni is ruining your safe space, you can start living"

Alex Proud

Ellis notes that he struggles to process being bullied online. I'm not sure I'd go quite that far, but I can tell you that being sent away to boarding school and bullied in real life is probably worse. And doubly so when all the adults around you think getting a good kicking is character-building.

On a more positive note, look at all the great stuff you have. I loved the 90s, but you found them insufferably boring. The internet barely existed. When we went travelling we took pictures using film and kept notes in diaries. We spent long stretches of time alone with our thoughts, unrelieved by tweets or posts.

Perhaps the reason we spent so much time in the pub (drinking filthy mass-produced lager, not craft ale) was because there was no

Netflix. Burgers were only ever dirty in a literal sense. There was no coffee culture. No Amazon. Maps not apps... Honestly, you'd think it was like living in boozy version of the Third World.

Anyway, as I say, I didn't thank my boomer friend when he gave me talk, but in the long term, I know he was right. And the main reason he was right is actually a really positive one. This is because the second you let go of the idea of having a perfect job or a loft in Shoreditch or the idea that the oppressive statue at uni is ruining your safe space, you can start living.

You quickly realise that you can be happy, despite not having everything you want. In fact, you realise that learning to put up with imperfections is what makes you happy.

I'm sure that in ten or 15 years time some of you will be having these thoughts about Generation Z. But that's the future.

This is now. And right now, you need to toughen up, grow up and stop being Generation Whine. You'll be a lot happier for it.

This article demonstrates that Generation X has taken upon themselves to same burdens as baby boomers, the perfectionist attitude that lingers with World War 2. We all make mistakes including Baby Boomers and Generation X and Millennials as well Kama Millennials have in the first to accept them in such a large scale. a classic Generation X response to this is to be tougher however, looking at statistics from all kinds of data the job market specifically, management is predominantly a job of Generation X so they use the strong boot attitude when hiring a millennial.

Chapter 4: Conclusion and self-discovery

In this chapter I want to discuss multiple learning moment that i have come to know.
I have interview for a position for property management, i brought along a resume with a display of my experience that i have 6 years of project management experience, the interviewer told me "I am not looking for a CEO." This struck me as an odd statement that he was making out of defense but it also gave

me an awareness of people having seen or afraid of the CEO.

This concept is pervasive with millennials because our parents and grandparents run business and we are either given a job or the job goes to the cheapest employee. This thought that a qualified person is corporate and want a hostile takeover shows a particular part of my job climate. The interviewer only displayed agitation when i asked how much this position pays. I have a strong feeling that this property management interviewer did not read my resume. I had a second similar offer and the only non- work related discussion was about if I knew my neighbors who were friends with the interviewer.

When i joined the real estate workplace i was hopeful and excited for a new day of life to get a chance to make money. I used to trust that if I was confident i would get what i want. I now hate making a phone call knowing full well the call would end with someone not interested. I hate work again. I am detoxing from trusting that thing will change or a random act of God would deliver me a paycheck.

In the process of the last 2 years i have come to accept that my fate is that i will not be paid money for my work. I am withdrawing from the expectation that i will make money period! I have been the victim of a scam involving fake checks with the prospect to do data entry. Connections seem to be a feature in employment for some. I have worked for free on a trial basis as a private construction inspector with hopes of employment and after what seemed like a good day. The owner said "you lack the experience but you are a nice guy." This was puzzling because he could not tell me which experience specifically. But i was comforted when i realized i would have been under appreciated so i am glad we are not working together. The reason of experience was certainly a cover up for a different reason.

    Another work experience comes to mind but before i discuss this i must add that many parts of my experience were personal to me and a healthy employee and employer experience is vital. An employer has the tendency to push for servitude. For instance, I worked as a teacher for a month and within that month the employer made reference to the color of my clothes as not fitting the position. I did not want to argue but after a few times of his persistent nagging I quit and told him that i am exploring other avenues of work. I gave him 2 weeks notice. 2 weeks after leaving I got a text from him that i am fired because we don't get along. He did know that i quit so i did not respond but the pathetic peripheral focus on is sues that don't pertain to the job is a truth.

In real estate i get little direction because i give the employer money if i produce. I don't make money no matter how hard i work period! There is irony there. I tried yoga and other sorts of introspective mediums to gain confidence but to no avail. No amounts of confidence have helped me thus far.

I went on an interview for a position in a financial firm in order to get a sponsor for my series 7, the interviewer asked me if i could make connections in the synagogue, i laughed and said no. He did not hire me. I have changed my mind's center from believing i would be rich by now to having nothing but debt and no belief in my getting paid. I thought it was me because of the pervasive issue but that is false. The economy does not have room to hire or my personality does not get paid.

I am not in despair rather i accept my fate of not making money. My job is to work with whatever is infront of me. The real estate business has been written and spoken about

ad nauseam with all that remains in my brain is that
it takes a long time to make money. I don't expect to make money at all but I still want to try the things that help others get money such as become a NYPD officer, write this book with a publisher and editor, and make cold-calls in real estate.

    Some time throughout my career thus far i have come to see the world as unjust. This is the truth but it does not affect my desire to work even it is unpaid. At low points i burn with jealousy and anger toward GOD who i used to place my trust in now i just believe that he could do everything. But he is in no rush to help me financially rather he want's me to squirm and desire all that is not mine and feel a deep emasculation and perhaps let other people earn reward for helping me.

    When i was getting paid I was very quick to spend my money and savings were far from any of my thoughts. Currently i want to fix my credit and purchase a home and other pieces of real estate to build for my sons future. I am broke and i believe no matter what i do i am cursed that i will not make money. I do work out of necessity.

The concept of working hard to get whatever you want is false. I do not look the part of a businessman because i have many visible tattoos. My goal is to demonstrate the fallacy to the work hard and you are guaranteed money.

In the book how capitalism will save us by Steve Forbes he says in the first page before the preface, "to the millions of individuals whose energy, innovation, and resilience built the Real World economy. Their enterprise, when unleashed, is always the answer." I agree intellectually but my experience today does not show me that hard work produces results monetarily.

I understand that many people fault find and blame others for failure, i know except that i will be living with my mom wife and son making no money despite working hard. There is no one to blame. I just want to live.

I went on an interview today with life insurance/investment bank. The interviewer was pleasant and we chatted for 1 hour. My assumption was that there is no salary in this job. I would primarily generate my own leads based upon the people i know. The thought had me uncomfortable, It would be months before i saw any money. The idea of salesperson would be how i make money. I have worked in a similar job where i was a representative of a company that sold lawyer services for a monthly payment. It felt like a waste of my time. I am not comfortable doing this work right now.

    This job is a 1 hour job from my home and there would be daily expenses that I could not afford. I am too far down into the red to take risks with my time. With my unjust luck i would not make money. I prefer to join the NYPD. Despite coming from a family where no one has done this, i am ready for this honorable work.

    The only offers i have are to work to create via sales to make money. Money that does not come to me. I no longer dream big rather live broke and with the reality that this is not changing. Despite my meditating on money coming to me. My family, wife, and grandparents were poor and so will I be.

    In summary I am one man who has seen many different sides to employment. At this point i will likely fail in earning money but i still do work. All the reasons that both myself and other think about are false in assessing my lack of getting paid. I suppose there is a time for everything including my failure monetarily.

Feel free to contact me with your experience on this journey.
        Samson Zelasko

www.ingramcontent.com/pod-product-compliance
Lightning Source LLC
Chambersburg PA
CBHW061440180526
45170CB00004B/1488